USING

MATHS

...IANTS

Wendy Clemson and David Clemson

ticktock

Copyright © ticktock Entertainment Ltd 2007
First published in Great Britain in 2007 by ticktock Media Ltd.,
Unit 2, Orchard Business Centre, North Farm Road,
Tunbridge Wells, Kent, TN2 3XF

ticktock project editor: Rebecca Clunes
ticktock project designer: Sara Greasley

ISBN 978 1 84696 058 1
Printed in China
A CIP catalogue record for this book is available from the British Library.

Picture credits
t=top, b=bottom, c=centre, l-left, r=right f=far
Lon E. Lauber, Alaska Image Library, United States Fish and Wildlife Service 10;
Mike Johnson/earthwindow.com 23; **IFAW International Fund for Animal Welfare/J. Gordon** 22L;
Kevin Raskoff, California State University, Monterey Bay/NOAA 14T; **David B Fleetham/SeaPics.com** 15, 19;
James D Watt/SeaPics.com 28-29B; **Richard Hermann/SeaPics.com** 18; **Bob Gibbons/Science Photo Library** 21;
Shutterstock 1, 2, 3FL, 3L, 3C, 3FR, 4TL, 4BL, 4BR, 5, 6, 8, 14B, 20L, 20R, 26, 27, 31T, 31B, 32;
age photostock/SuperStock 3R, 11, 17T, 24-25, 30B; **Alan Briere/SuperStock** 13B;
Ticktock Media archives 3L, 13T, 17B, 22R; **U.S. Army** 4TR
All cover images by Shutterstock except front cover shark image, from Carl Roessler/Getty

Contents

Under the Ocean

You have an exciting job. You're a deep sea diver. You explore amazing underwater worlds, full of giant creatures. You see enormous fish, octopus and whales during your dives. You travel all over the world, diving in warm and cold waters. It's time to start off on a new trip!

Being a deep sea diver is an exciting and important job.

A diver sometimes has to look for a sunken ship and find out what made it sink.

Sometimes, pipes and ships need to be fixed underwater.

Divers can be scientists who study fish, plants, rocks and ocean water.

Divers take pictures underwater. The pictures are used in films, tv programmes and adverts.

But did you know that deep sea divers sometimes have to use maths?

Inside this book you will find maths activities that divers have to do all the time. There are also lots of number puzzles about ocean animals.

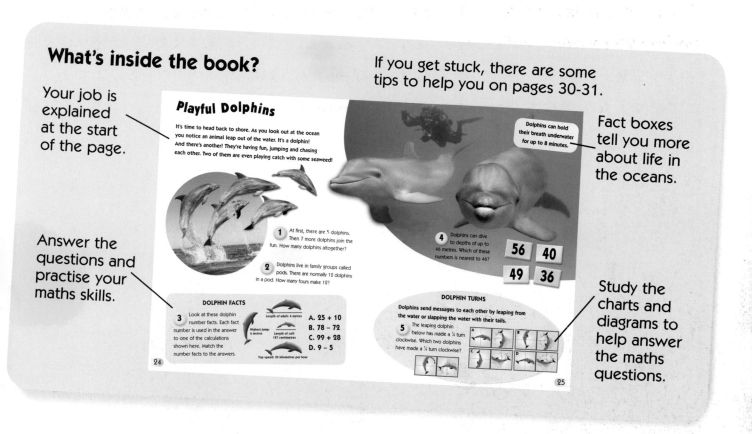

What's inside the book?

Your job is explained at the start of the page.

Answer the questions and practise your maths skills.

If you get stuck, there are some tips to help you on pages 30-31.

Fact boxes tell you more about life in the oceans.

Study the charts and diagrams to help answer the maths questions.

Playful Dolphins

It's time to head back to shore. As you look out at the ocean you notice an animal leap out of the water. It's a dolphin! And there's another! They're having fun, jumping and chasing each other. Two of them are even playing catch with some seaweed!

Dolphins can hold their breath underwater for up to 8 minutes.

1 At first, there are 5 dolphins. Then 7 more dolphins join the fun. How many dolphins altogether?

2 Dolphins live in family groups called pods. There are normally 12 dolphins in a pod. How many fours make 12?

4 Dolphins can dive to depths of up to 46 metres. Which of these numbers is nearest to 46?

56   40
49   36

DOLPHIN FACTS

3 Look at these dolphin number facts. Each fact number is used in the answer to one of the calculations shown here. Match the number facts to the answers.

Length of adult: 4 metres
Highest jump: 6 metres
Length of calf: 157 centimetres
Top speed: 35 kilometres per hour

A. 25 + 10
B. 78 − 72
C. 99 + 28
D. 9 − 5

DOLPHIN TURNS

Dolphins send messages to each other by leaping from the water or slapping the water with their tails.

5 The leaping dolphin below has made a ¼ turn clockwise. Which two dolphins have made a ¼ turn clockwise?

24

25

Are you ready to be a deep sea diver?

You will need paper, a pen, a ruler and don't forget to bring your diving suit! Let's go...

Going Diving

The ocean is cold. You need to wear a thick wetsuit to keep you warm. You also wear a mask and thick boots. An air tank on your back lets you breathe underwater. Lead weights stop you from floating upwards!

In this box is some of your diving equipment.

1 Is the air hose higher or lower than the air tanks?

no

2 What is to the right of the flippers?

3 What is directly above the face mask?

The air hose

DIVING EQUIPMENT

Air hose   Flippers   Lead weights

Face mask   Air tanks

Most dives last about an hour, but some jobs take longer. You could be underwater for two, three or even four hours.

You see lots of creatures underwater. You can keep a record of what you see under the water on a map like this.

UNDERWATER MAP

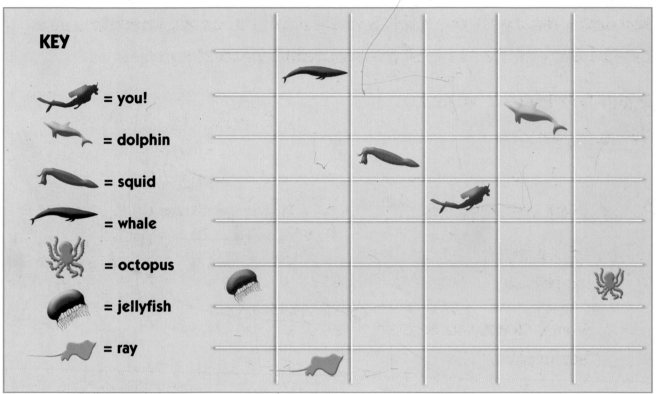

KEY

= you!

= dolphin

= squid

= whale

= octopus

= jellyfish

= ray

Use the Underwater Map to answer these questions. To reach the dolphin, you have to move 2 squares up and 1 square right (another way of getting there is to move 1 square right and 2 squares up).

4 How would you move to reach the whale?
3 up 2 sideways

5 How would you move to get to the jellyfish?
2 down 3 sideways

6 The ray is 4 squares down and 2 squares right from you – true or false?

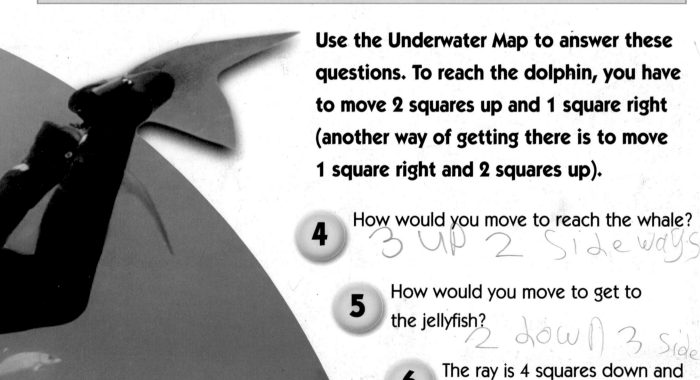

Supertankers and big ships

You are on a ship that will take you to your diving spot. You look out over the ocean and see a supertanker. This is a ship that carries barrels of oil around the world. Supertankers are huge. They are man-made ocean giants!

Here are the biggest ships you have seen.

1 Which is the longest ship?

2 How many ships are longer than the Ronald Reagan?

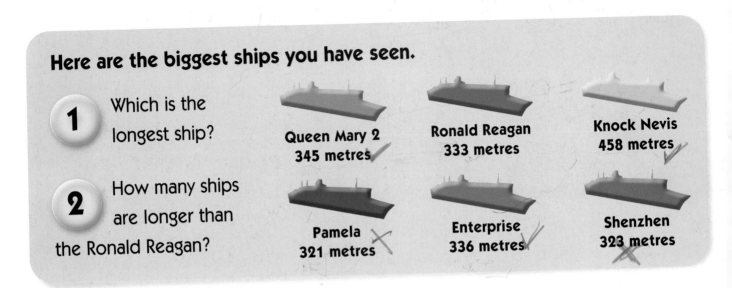

Queen Mary 2
345 metres

Ronald Reagan
333 metres

Knock Nevis
458 metres

Pamela
321 metres

Enterprise
336 metres

Shenzhen
323 metres

The speed of a ship is measured in knots. One knot is about 2 kilometres per hour, so a ship travelling at 30 knots is going about 60 kilometres per hour.

SHIP SPEED CHART

Name of ship	Speed in knots
Queen Mary 2	30
Pamela	26
Ronald Reagan	30
Enterprise	33½
Knock Nevis	16
Shenzhen	25

3 Which is the fastest ship?

4 Which ships go at the same speed?

5 Look at this chart and the ships on page 8. Is the longest ship also the slowest?

Supertankers are the biggest ships in the world. They can be nearly half a kilometre long.

NORDSTRAUM

North Pole Animal

Your ship heads to the sea near the North Pole. You have been asked to study sea lions and walruses here. You need to find out how deep they dive and what they eat. You discover that these animals are even better at diving than you are!

Sea lions gather near the shore, so they don't have far to go to get into the water.

1 Sea lions can stay underwater for 40 minutes. One sea lion has been under water for 18 minutes. How much longer can it stay under the sea?

2 Sea lions can dive 240 metres under the water. During your dive you spot a sea lion 40 metres under the sea. How much further down can it go?

Male sea lions are about 3 metres long and weigh about a tonne.

Male walruses can be 3½ metres long and weigh over 1½ tonnes.

WHAT DID A WALRUS EAT?

You spend a few days watching a walrus. Here is a block graph of what it eats.

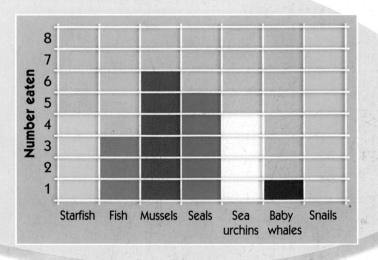

Number eaten

Starfish · Fish · Mussels · Seals · Sea urchins · Baby whales · Snails

3 How many snails did the walrus eat?

4 Which creatures did it eat four of?

5 What is the difference between the number of fish and seals?

6 How many creatures did it eat in total?

Avoiding the Jellyfish

It's time to get back into the icy water. You're diving to find one of the world's largest jellyfish. It is the lion's mane jellyfish. You don't have to dive down far before you spot the jellyfish. It is very big, almost the size of you. You stay far away from its tentacles, if they touch your skin they will sting!

1 There are lots of different types of jellyfish to be found in this ocean. You draw a picture of some different types. You draw lines to show which jellyfish belong to the same group. What shapes have you drawn?

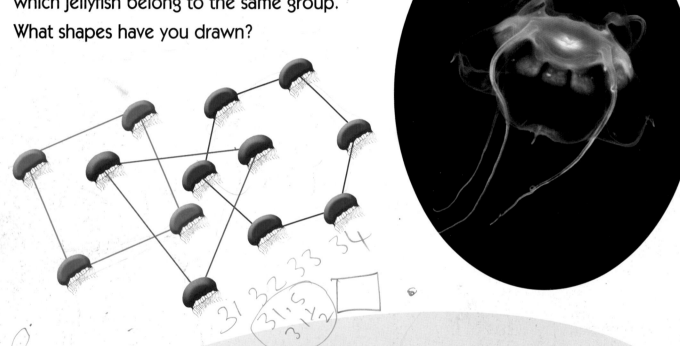

31 32 33 34
31.5
31½

The lion's mane jellyfish has long floating tentacles. They can be more than 35 metres long.

2 What are the whole numbers that can fit between 30 and 35?

3 How many fives are there in 35?

4 A lion's mane jellyfish lives for about a year. How many days is that?

5 You see a lion's mane jellyfish that is about 2 months old. Approximately how many days old is it?

A jellyfish doesn't have a brain, heart, eyes, ears or bones.

Shark Attack!

Your next job is going to take you to the other side of the world. You've been asked to collect information on sharks. They live in warmer waters, so you leave the North Pole and head south. Some sharks attack humans, so you don't want to dive. Instead, you collect the information safely from your boat.

SHARK LENGTH GRAPH

Boat

Shark

0 1 2 3 4 5 6 7 8 9 10 11
Metres

1 The graph shows a shark swimming beside your boat. How long is the shark?

2 What is the difference in length between your boat and the shark?

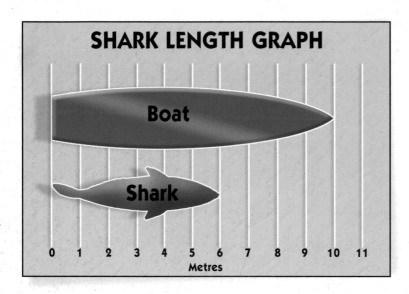

SHARK MEASUREMENT CHART

Hammerhead shark
4 metres

Basking shark
10 metres

Megamouth shark
4½ metres

Whale shark
12 metres

Great white shark
6 metres

3 Which sharks in this picture are longer than the great white shark?

4 Put the five sharks in order of length, from the longest to the shortest.

5 You put some bait into the water and wait. Suddenly a great white shark bursts from the water. As it grabs the bait you look at its razor-sharp teeth. You count the teeth you can see. It has 26 at the top and 24 at the bottom. How many teeth does it have in total?

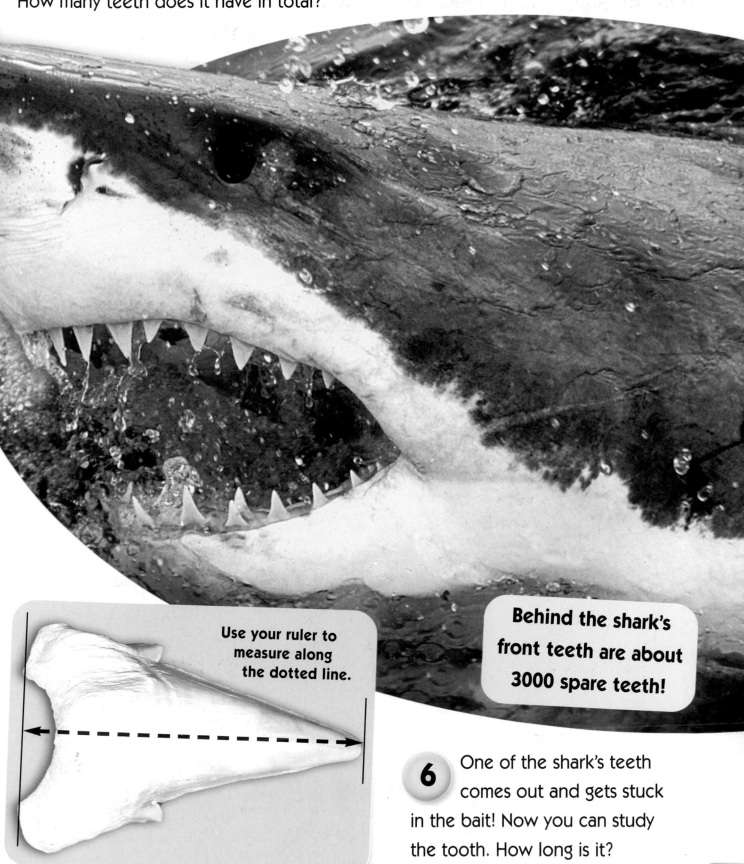

Use your ruler to measure along the dotted line.

Behind the shark's front teeth are about 3000 spare teeth!

6 One of the shark's teeth comes out and gets stuck in the bait! Now you can study the tooth. How long is it?

Giant Octopus and Squid

You now head away from the coast, into deeper waters. You are looking for two of the most mysterious creatures of the ocean: the giant octopus and the colossal squid. The giant octopus isn't seen much, and the colossal squid has never been seen alive. You might be lucky, and see both!

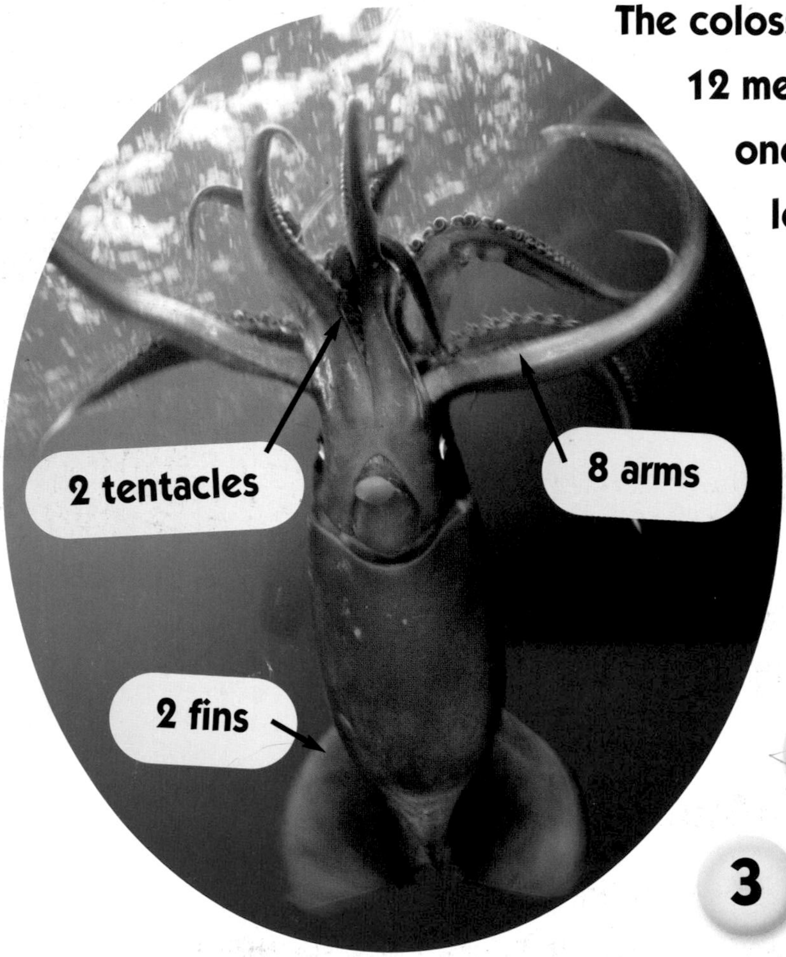

The colossal squid is probably about 12 metres long. No scientist has seen one alive, but they can guess its length from the remains of colossal squid found in whales' stomachs. They know it looks similar to the squid seen here.

2 tentacles

8 arms

2 fins

1 How many fins are there on 4 squids?

2 How many tentacles are there on 7 squids?

3 How many arms are there on 2 squids?

LONGER THAN A MINIBUS

4 Some squid are the size of two minibuses. Look at this row of minibuses. How many squids would this measure?

The giant octopus can grow up to 5 metres long.

Not only is the giant octopus long, it also weighs a lot.

Some have been found to weigh up to 180 kilograms!

OCTOPUS DIAGRAM

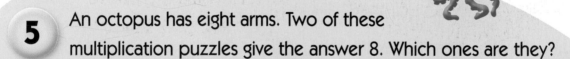

5 An octopus has eight arms. Two of these multiplication puzzles give the answer 8. Which ones are they?

2 x 6 =

4 x 4 =

8 x 1 =

4 x 2 =

8 x 10 =

3 x 3 =

6 You can also make eight by adding two numbers. What are the ways of adding two numbers to make 8?

For the last few weeks you've been far from land, out at sea. Suddenly you spot a wandering albatross – the biggest sea bird in the world. You are hundreds of miles from the nearest shore, but that doesn't worry the albatross. It spends years at sea without stopping on land.

A bird's wingspan is measured from the tip of one wing to the tip of the other. The wandering albatross can have a wingspan of 2½ metres.

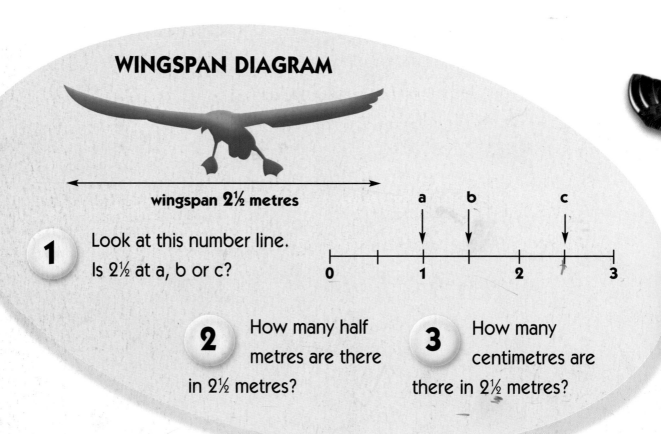

WINGSPAN DIAGRAM

wingspan 2½ metres

1 Look at this number line. Is 2½ at a, b or c?

2 How many half metres are there in 2½ metres?

3 How many centimetres are there in 2½ metres?

The wandering albatross is a big bird, and it lays big eggs too. Its egg is about 10 centimetres high. That's the height of a soup tin!

10 centimetres

Scientists sometimes put tags on the birds to track them and learn more about them. You see five tagged birds. The tags tell you how old each bird is. Here are their ages.

A 22 years   B 38 years   C 14 years   D 7 years   E 23 years

4 Can you round each bird's age up or down, to the nearest 10?

10 20 30 40 50 60 70 80 90 100

35

The wandering albatross can live up to 80 years.

The Manta Ray

Your boat stops near a coral reef. This is a sea-garden made from the skeletons of tiny sea animals. The water here is warm and brightly coloured fish swim around you. Suddenly a giant shadow passes over you. It's a manta ray! It must be at least 7 metres wide.

You've been asked to find out how big the manta rays swimming around you are. You catch some in a net to weigh and measure. Here are your results.

	Width	Weight
Ray 1	4½ m	500 kg
Ray 2	5½ m	1000 kg
Ray 3	6 m	1500 kg

1 Which ray weighs the most?

2 What is the difference in width between Ray 1 and Ray 3?

3 What is the difference in weight between Ray 1 and Ray 2?

4 If this manta ray turns around in a half circle, which picture shows how it will look?

— eyes

— fins

— tail

A

B

C

Manta rays swim near the surface of the water. They feed on tiny sea creatures. They are not usually a danger to humans.

27

Your Last Dive

You've carried out diving jobs all around the world. This is the last one of your trip. The coral reef is home to many animals. You look around and see lots of tiny, brightly coloured fish darting about. As you watch, a giant group of fish swims by. The group, called a shoal, twists and turns together, almost as if they are one big fish. This confuses hunters.

BLUE AND GREEN FISH

A shoal has lots of fish in it. Here is a diagram of the shoal that you see.

1 How many fish are blue?

2 How many fish are green?

3 How many fish are blue and green?

FISH CHART

4 You have made a chart of the number of shoals you have seen on each dive. On which dive did you see most shoals?

5 How many shoals did you see altogether?

6 How many shoals of fish did you see on Dive 2?

KEY

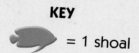 = 1 shoal

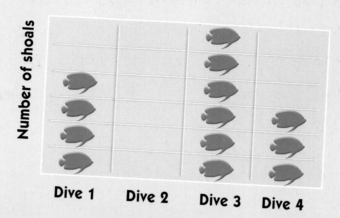

Number of shoals

Dive 1　　Dive 2　　Dive 3　　Dive 4

It's time to head back to shore. But diving is fun! You'll be back in the water soon.

Tips and Help

PAGES 6-7

Grid maps – You can work out the routes on a grid map by moving right or left and up or down (or up or down and then right or left).

PAGES 8-9

Comparing and ordering – To put numbers like this in order, look at the hundreds, the tens and finally the units or ones.

PAGES 10-11

Subtracting (taking away) – Look for ways to make this easier to do. For example, 40 take away 18 can be done as 40 take away 20 leaves 20 add 2 giving the answer 22.

Block graph – Each coloured 'block' in the graph means one creature that was eaten. A block graph helps us to compare two sets of information (here, these are how many of each creature was eaten).

Find the difference – This is the same as 'take away', 'minus' or 'subtract'.

PAGES 12-13

Predicting patterns – When we work out how a pattern would continue we are predicting (guessing what will happen). Count the squares, look for a pattern; then imagine the same pattern goes on across the page.

PAGES 14-15

Numbers between – Picture a number line to help you. Then you can see the missing numbers.

Flat shapes – Counting the sides is necessary in naming flat shapes. A triangle has three sides, a hexagon six sides and a rectangle four sides (opposite sides match in length) and four right angles.

Fives in 35 – Write down all of the 'fives' that will fit in 35: 5, 10, 15, 20 and so on. Then count up the numbers you have written.

PAGES 16-17

Ordering length – First check that all the things are measured using the same unit of measurement (here they are all in metres). Look to see which have tens (whale shark and basking shark). Then check the units. The whale shark also has 2 units so this is the longest. Now put those without tens in order.

Using a ruler – Make sure the '0' on the ruler is exactly on one end of the line to measure. Then you can 'read off' what the scale on the ruler says at the other end of the line.

PAGES 18-19

Multiplication – Multiplication is the same as 'times' or 'lots of'. We use the sign 'x' to mean times. 4 x 2 is the same as 4 lots of 2.

PAGES 20-21

Rounding numbers – When we round a number to the nearest ten we make a number ending in 5, 6, 7, 8 or 9 bigger and numbers ending in 1, 2, 3 or 4 smaller. So 22 rounded to the nearest ten is 20, whereas 38 becomes 40 because it is rounded up.

PAGES 22-23

Maths signs – Remember what the maths signs mean:
+ means add, plus or sum
– means take away, minus or subtract
x means multiply by or times
÷ means share by or divide by

Measures – Remember we use litres and millilitres to measure liquids, kilograms and grams to measure weight and kilometres, metres and centimetres to measure length.

Timing – If you swim 5 metres in 10 seconds, you swim 7 x 5 metres in 7 x 10 seconds.

PAGES 24-25

Nearest numbers – Count on and back from 46. Which number do you reach soonest? That is the number nearest to 46.

Clockwise – This is the way the hands on a clock move around.

PAGES 26-27

Width – When we measure the size of something we can look at its length (or height) and width.

Turning around – A full circle is one complete turn.

PAGES 28-29

Sorting – This is called a Venn diagram. It shows a set of fish with blue on them and a set of fish with green on them. The sets overlap so that the fish with both blue and green on them are in the blue set and in the green set.

Pictogram – This is a chart where a picture is used as a symbol for information. In this pictogram a fish shape means one shoal.

Answers

PAGES 6-7

1 higher
2 lead weights
3 air hose
4 three squares up, two squares left
5 two squares down, three squares left
6 false – it is four squares down, two squares left

PAGES 8-9

1 Knock Nevis
2 3 ships
3 Enterprise
4 Queen Mary 2 and Ronald Reagan
5 yes

PAGES 10-11

1 22 minutes
2 200 metres
3 8 snails
4 starfish and sea urchins
5 2
6 31 animals

PAGES 12-13

1 5 minutes
2 2 kilometres
3 A white
  B white
  C black
  D white
4 12 orcas

PAGES 14-15

1 square, triangle and hexagon
2 31, 32, 33 and 34
3 7
4 365 days
5 about 60 days

PAGES 16-17

1 6 metres
2 4 metres
3 whale shark and basking shark
4 whale shark, basking shark, great white shark, megamouth shark, hammerhead shark
5 50 teeth
6 9 centimetres

PAGES 18-19

1 8 fins
2 14 tentacles
3 16 arms
4 2½ squids
5 4 x 2 and 8 x 1
6 0+8, 8+0, 1+7, 7+1, 2+6, 6+2, 3+5, 5+3, 4+4

PAGES 20-21

1 c
2 5
3 250 centimetres
4 A 20, B 40, C10, D 10, E 20

PAGES 22-23

1 minke whale – 8 metres long
2 10 groups of 5
3 25 pairs
4 A 33 metres
  B 4000 kilograms
  C 100 litres
5 70 seconds, or 1 minute and 10 seconds

PAGES 24-25

1 12 dolphins
2 3
3 A top speed
  B highest jump
  C Length of calf
  D Length of adult
4 49
5 A and C

PAGES 26-27

1 Ray 3
2 1½ metres
3 500 kilograms
4 B

PAGES 28-29

1 9 blue fish
2 17 green fish
3 6 blue and green fish
4 dive 3
5 13 shoals of fish
6 zero (0) shoals